Friends For Life

Deborah Ewing and Noreen Ramsden

Illustrated by Paddy Bouma

Maria was frightened of Busi and the other big girls. She put her head down and walked past them – but she bumped straight into Busi!

Busi dropped the book she was carrying and shouted.

'You silly girl – look what you did! Pick up my book.'

Maria picked up the book.

Busi shouted, 'Look, you've torn it – you'll have to pay for it!'

Busi's friends started to sing. 'Make her pay, pay, pay!'

One of the girls snatched Maria's school bag. Maria tried to pull it back. She slipped and cut her knee.

Just then Samuel walked up, and the big girls moved away.

'Are you all right, M?' he asked Maria. He gave her a tissue.

'Stop the bleeding by pressing on the cut,' he said. Then he walked off to the soccer field.

Later, Maria saw a crowd of boys cheering Samuel because he had scored a goal. He looked very happy.

But then Maria heard Busi and her friends talking about Samuel.

'His mother is very sick. My Aunty says she is as thin as a broomstick. She didn't say what was wrong but people say it must be AIDS.'

A heavy feeling came over Maria. 'Poor Samuel,' she thought.

When Maria arrived home she cried, and her Mama asked what was wrong. Maria told her about the bullying and her cut knee.

'You know,' said Mama, 'bullies are very weak people. If you show you are angry or sad, they feel powerful. If you take no notice of the teasing, they don't have any power.'

A few days later, the Principal told the school that Samuel's mother had died.

'This is very sad. Everyone must be kind to Samuel when he comes back to school after the funeral. It is a very hard thing to lose your mother.'

The Principal did not say the word AIDS but Maria heard children whispering the word. Some of them laughed in an unkind way when they said 'AIDS'.

'What is AIDS?' Maria asked her mother.

'AIDS is sickness that comes from a virus called HIV. This virus weakens the body so that it can't fight illness. When a person who has the virus gets very sick, it is called AIDS,' answered her mother.

'I used Sam's tissue – will I catch AIDS?' asked Maria.

'Not from using his tissues,' said her mother. 'People usually get AIDS through having sex with someone who has the virus in their body. You cannot catch AIDS like you catch flu!'

Maria hugged her mother and thought about Samuel. He didn't have a mother now.

'Why must people die?' Maria sobbed.

'Everyone is born and lives their life,' said Mama. 'Then the time comes to die. No one knows when it will happen. That's why every moment we live is precious.

'We must fill our lives with love and kindness. Then we will always have good memories to help us through difficult times.'

Samuel came back to school looking very sad and thin. No one in his class wanted to sit next to him. Busi whispered to her friends that Samuel must have AIDS too.

After school, Maria saw two boys from the soccer team push Sam. They made him drop his bag. They called him an orphan.

'Stay away from school or you will give us AIDS!' they said.

Samuel did not lose his temper. He just said, 'Don't forget that anyone can become an orphan – even you.'

Maria ran up to Sam and said, 'They talk nonsense. I know you can't catch AIDS like flu!'

Sam smiled. 'Thanks, M!'

Maria helped Sam pick up the things that had fallen from his bag. There was a photo of a woman smiling.

'That is my Mama,' he said. 'And this was our favourite book. I call these special things my family treasures. I'm going to put them in a box.'

'That's a great idea, Sam,' said Maria.

The Principal was standing nearby. He thought it was a great idea too …

The next day the Principal spoke to all the school.

'You might have heard of Nkosi Johnson. He won the World Children's Prize in 2002, for speaking out about living with HIV/AIDS. We have someone brave like Nkosi in our school and he has an important message for you.'

Samuel came forward. He said, 'You all know that my Mother has died. She had AIDS. Before she died she gave me this box. Inside are our family treasures, our precious things. They remind me of my mother. They remind me of who I am and where I come from. They are a way of keeping the happy times we spent together.

'Bad things happen to all of us. Happy memories help us to be brave.'

The Principal started clapping. Everyone clapped. And Maria clapped loudest of all.

At home, Maria found an old straw basket.

'Can I have this for our family treasures?' she asked her Mama.

'I didn't know we had any family treasures,' laughed Mama.

'We've got lots,' said Maria. 'Look what I've found.'

The next day at school Maria called to Sam, 'Look, Sam, I have my own family treasures!'

'Did your Mama die too?' Samuel asked.

'No,' said Maria. 'I am making a basketful of happy memories NOW. Life is precious.'

Samuel replied, 'Friends are precious too. We can be friends for life.'

Let's talk

How do you feel when someone calls you bad names?

What did Sam do when he was called bad names?

Why do you think some of the children laughed when they talked about AIDS?

How do you think we should treat our friends who have AIDS?

How can we help children who have been orphaned to feel better?

If you had a box for your family treasures, what would you put in it?